ADVENTURES IN CULTURE

CELEBRATIONS
AROUND THE WORLD

By Charles Murphy

Gareth Stevens
PUBLISHING

Please visit our website, www.garethstevens.com. For a free color catalog of all our high-quality books, call toll free 1-800-542-2595 or fax 1-877-542-2596.

Cataloging-in-Publication Data

Names: Murphy, Charles.
Title: Celebrations around the world / Charles Murphy.
Description: New York : Gareth Stevens Publishing, 2017. | Series: Adventures in culture | Includes index.
Identifiers: ISBN 9781482455755 (pbk.) | ISBN 9781482455779 (library bound) | ISBN 9781482455762 (6 pack)
Subjects: LCSH: Holidays–Cross-cultural studies–Juvenile literature. | Special days–Cross-cultural studies–Juvenile literature.
Classification: LCC GT3933.M87 2017 | DDC 394.26–dc23

Published in 2017 by
Gareth Stevens Publishing
111 East 14th Street, Suite 349
New York, NY 10003

Designer: Andrea Davison-Bartolotta and Bethany Perl
Editor: Therese Shea

Photo credits: Cover, p. 1 gagarych/Shutterstock.com; pp. 2-24 (background texture) Flas100/Shutterstock.com; p. 5 wavebreakmedia/Shutterstock.com; p. 7 Kobby Dagan/Shutterstock.com; p. 9 Anthony Pappone/Moment/Getty Images; p. 11 123Nelson/Shutterstock.com; p. 13 T photography/Shutterstock.com; p. 15 Atid Kiattisaksiri/LightRocket/Getty Images; p. 17 GUILLERMO LEGARIA/AFP/Getty Images; p. 19 Iakov Filimonov/Shutterstock.com; p. 21 The Asahi Shimbun/The Asahi Shimbun/Getty Images.

Printed in China

CPSIA compliance information: Batch #CW17GS: For further information contact Gareth Stevens, New York, New York at 1-800-542-2595.

CONTENTS

Boldface words appear in the glossary.

It's Party Time!

Do you love parties? Your family, school, and community probably have many special **celebrations**. They might celebrate Halloween, Christmas, the Fourth of July, and birthdays. Many **cultures** around the world celebrate special times in special ways, too.

5

Day of the Dead

Day of the Dead is called Día de los Muertos (DEE-ah DEH LOHS MUEHR-tohs) in Spanish. It's mostly celebrated in Mexico and other parts of **Latin America** to honor loved ones who have died. It's a special day of food and gifts!

Festima

West Africans come together each February for Festima. This **festival** in the country of Burkina Faso celebrates African masks. Masks made of leaves, straw, wood, or other matter have been used in Africa for thousands of years to honor **ancestors** and spirits.

Chinese New Year

Chinese New Year begins between January 21 and February 20. It lasts 15 days! During that time, people visit family. They dress in red colors and watch fireworks. There may be a parade with a long dragon, a **symbol** of good luck.

11

Carnival

Carnival is a spring festival around the world. In Switzerland, people ring bells to celebrate the end of winter. In Italy, people wear **costumes**. The most famous Carnival may be in Rio de Janeiro, Brazil. It has music, parades, and dancing.

13

Loy Krathong

Loy Krathong (LOY krah-TOHNG) is celebrated throughout Thailand in Southeast Asia. Thousands of people free paper **lanterns** into the sky. Others float lanterns of candles and flowers down rivers. They ask for good luck.

15

La Tomatina

The town of Buñol in Spain holds a festival called La Tomatina (LAH toh-mah-TEE-nah). Thousands of people throw tomatoes at each other! No one is sure how the festival began. Now, about 20,000 people each August join this giant food fight.

Holi

Holi (HOH-lee) is a spring festival celebrated in India in February or March. Sometimes it's called the Festival of Colors. People celebrate for **religious** reasons and to welcome spring. They throw colored water or powder as part of the fun!

19

Obon

Obon (oh-BOHN) is a festival celebrated in Japan in July or August. It's a time to honor ancestors. People light lanterns and float them in water. They also perform a special dance called the Bon-Odori. Which festival would you like to celebrate?

INDEX